A Different Thousand and One Nights

Titus Naso

Tomis Press

A Different Thousand and One Nights
Copyright ©2024 by Titus Naso

All rights reserved. No part of this publication may be reproduced, performed, or stored in a retrieval system, shared, or transmitted in any form or by any means, without the express written permission of the publisher.

Published by Tomis Press
Silverton, Oregon

Hardcover ISBN: 978-1-958337-07-3
Paperback ISBN: 978-1-958337-24-0
E-Book ISBN: 978-1-958337-25-7

First printing November 8, 2024

The poems "Johnny Appleseed" and "Casey Jones" were previously published in the Tomis Press collection, *The Histories: Selected Poems from Annum Poetica* by Titus Naso, ©2023.

"The Fruit Seller's Tale" was previously published in the Tomis Press collection, *Choosing Change* by Titus Naso, ©2023.

This book is a derivative work based on a larger work previously copyrighted under the title, *Annum Poetica*, Copyright ©2021 by Titus Naso.

Cover photograph ©2001 by Jesse S. Smith.

Titus Naso is a pen name of Jesse S. Smith.

titusnaso.com • tomispress.com • jessesmithbooks.com

Poetry / Mythology & Folk Tales / Adult Humor

Contents

Introduction	5
The Tale of Sheherazade's Sister	9
Dorothy and the Wizard of Oz	15
Johnny Appleseed	19
Paul Bunyan	21
John Henry	22
Moby Dick	23
Alice in Wonderland	25
Casey Jones	33
Sherlock Holmes	36
The Headless Horseman of Sleepy Hollow	37
Cinderella	42
A Christmas Carol	44
The Fruit Seller's Tale	46
Rip van Winkle	47
The Bremen Town Musicians	55
Bre'er Rabbit	60
Gigantomachy	63
The Trojan War, Part 1	73
Dunyazade's Epilogue	81
References	85

Introduction

    I suppose I should note first of all that these poems contain adult situations and themes, and may not be suitable for children.

    And based on reader feedback it seems I should make doubly clear that "Titus Naso" is merely an amusing pen name for a poet who considers himself both modern and common.

    Right, with that out of the way, let's have some fun.

    The first thirteen poems in the present collection were written as part of my "year of poetry" challenge. As my favorite readers know, I challenged myself to write a poem a day, each day for a year, from April 2020 to April 2021. That year's creative output has already yielded the first four volumes in this *Annum Poetica* series: namely, *Months and Days*, *A Year Outside of Time*, *The Histories*, and *Choosing Change*.

    Although that initial "year of poetry" concluded in April of 2021, I continued adding new poems to this particular collection through October of 2022. And there are still many more poems I would love to add! But at some point I had to admit to myself that this is as complete as it's going to get for the time being. If fortune smiles upon me, then perhaps someday I may release an updated version of the *Nights* that adds another group of wickedly delicious modern takes to the collection. For now, it's time to share this existing material with you, dear reader.

    So, with that said, I hope the reader will enjoy the present collection for what it is, rather than dwelling overmuch on what it lacks; and I hope these fresh if perhaps sometimes offensive takes on familiar tales and themes will bring you delight and wonder. Failing that, I hope you have a good sense of humor. Cheers!

    ~Titus Naso
    October 1, 2024

The Frame

The Tale of Scheherazade's Sister

Broad were the leaves of the stately palm trees
lining the road to the royal palace
with its golden-domed minarets gleaming,
its walls of marble, and archways ornate:
a palace of luxury and great wealth
paid for by the working poor of the land.

Alas, the sheikh who lived therein saw not
the splendor of his great fortune and wealth,
the costly tapestries and silk pillows
adorning spacious walls and furniture;
his mind, instead, consumed with bitter rage,
the darkness of the thoughts in which he dwelt:
for he had been deceived by one he loved.
The pain of it still festered in his mind,
as an infection festers in the flesh
when a deep wound is not cleaned out in time,
causing abscess which putrefies and spreads,
'til body whole with fever is consumed:
just so his mind was consumed with his pain,
which he took out upon all those around.

The sheikh decreed that, since he'd lost his love,
a new wife he would marry ev'ry day;
and in the morning each of them behead,
so he would never get attached again:
for he was so consumed by bitterness
that he had ceased to regard other's lives,
but only saw in them means to an end.
Since one had hurt him, he would hurt them all!
This was his plan; and so much pow'r had he
that none could gainsay him, nor put an end
to evil plans that would cause suffering –
so evil is authoritarian rule.

Although unpopular was this decree,
in his kingdom, his pow'r was absolute.
Many innocent women murdered he:
no, there was no excuse for him, the brute.
At last, all of the pretty ones were dead,
or else they with their families had fled.

Now his advisor, who'd enabled him
by finding a new victim ev'ry day,
at last must bear some consequence for guilt
when he could offer Sheikh no other prey,
so offered his own daughter for the kill;
he was quite bummed, but saw no other way.
(Had Jafar been a competent vizier,
  he'd sooner begged the sheikh, "Forbear to slay
    so many innocents!" – and yet this thought
  had not occurred to him, it's sad to say.)

The elder sister, named Scheherazade,
is famous for her part in this grim tale.
The younger sister much forgotten is,
although her voice Scheherazade did save.

For Dunyazade (this was the sister's name)
begged entrance to the royal chamber first,
so she could bid Scheherazade farewell
and be with her upon her wedding night.
Then sat she by the bed's foot, on the floor,
and listened while her big sister... you know:
the moans and groans and rutting sweaty sounds
the couple made as they their pleasure took.
Poor Dunyazade sat there, quiet the while,
and thought how this night would come to an end:
at dawn, the sheikh Scheherazade beheads!
At last, panting and moaning slowed apace,
and Dunyazade, full tremulous with fear,

addressed herself to coupling's afterglow:
"Scheherazade, I beg you, will you tell
  a story to us, to pass these dark hours,
  so that we might on happier thoughts dwell
  and satisfy imagination's powers?"

Scheherazade assented, and began
the first of many stories to narrate.
Throughout the ev'ning strange, her story ran
until the hour was early, 'twas so late.
The sun was rising in the Eastern sky,
the hour neared when Scheherazade must die,
and yet the story long had not been told.
Then Dunyazade quite weary, with a sigh
said, "Sister, I'm sorry to interrupt,
  but I cannot open my weary eyes.
  Glad as I am that you at least got fucked,
  it seems a shame that you will have to die
  before you finish telling your story
  to your mass-murd'ring husband, and to me."

The sheikh just shrugged his shoulders with a yawn,
and turned his back unto the rising dawn.
"The story you can tell tonight instead;
  tomorrow's just as good to chop your head."

And in this way, a habit those three formed,
that lasted for a Thousand and One nights:
after the couple fucked and looked at porn,
Sheherazade told stories 'til the light,
always with Dunyazade prodding her on:
that Arab sister, praised be she in song!

What follows are the stories that she told:
Sheherazade, who was so very bold.
And as she whispered tales to the night air,
her sister Dunyazade was always there.

The Tales

Dorothy and the Wizard of Oz

So fierce was the storm that it tore a hole
right through the fabric of reality.
It tore up the trees and hedges, sheds and barns,
and it tore up Dorothy's country farmhouse.
There she was hiding with Toto, her dog,
when the house was ripped from its foundations
and flung far a-sky above the farm fields
spinning round and round in a way houses
are never supposed to spin. The frightened girl
was sure she'd met her doom, and expected
at any moment to be crushed to death.

A giant monster was the roaring wind,
the rav'ning maw of whirlpool Charybdis
and Dorothy's house a piece of flotsam, caught
in the fierce inescapable current
like the doomed ship of brave Odysseus
who to a bough clung while companions died.
Dorothy, having no such bough within reach,
took shelter underneath her bed, the dog
huddled against her for comfort, frightened.
Each second lasted an eternity
as they hid under the bed from the storm
expecting at any moment to die.

At last the wind slowed, the air pressure dropped;
the house, suddenly unsupported, fell
plummeting to the earth, and landed hard
with a shuddering crash that crushed the walls,
and all the remaining windows were shattered;

the dishes in the china cabinet broke,
the framed painting fell clatt'ring to the floor.
Too terrified to scream, Dorothy covered
her head with her hands, expecting the end.
The dog licked her face. Somehow they had lived!

The rest of the story is now well-known,
how Dorothy met up with an evil witch
who introduced herself as "Glenda the Good."
This Glenda congratulated Dorothy,
whose house had accidentally murdered
the law-abiding Governor Eastwitch,
who had been trying to talk some reason
into the insurrectionist Munchkins
who liked nothing better than to riot,
tearing up bricks from the Yellow Brick Road
and hurling them willy-nilly about
the way a dirty monkey flings its poo.
Now, with the Governor dead, the Munchkins
were free to indulge their anarchist ways,
stealing valuables, burning down houses.
What, you thought you heard a different version?
The victors write the history books, you know,
and always grant themselves heroic roles.
So toxic was Glenda (self-styled "The Good")
that she refused to tell Dorothy the truth
about the magic slippers on her feet,
instead assigning her an errand fraught
whereby she would meet danger, maybe death.

Brave Dorothy walked the road of yellow bricks
alone but for Toto, her little dog.
Along their journey they met some weirdos:
the brainless Scarecrow, straw-stuffed farmer;
the heartless clear-cut logger, Tin Woodsman;
the savage bully, Cowardly Lion.

When they arrived at Emerald City,
they thought the Mayor would solve their problems –
they did not realize he was a fraud.
Mayor Oz would not admit to his lies.
Rather than confess his deception,
he sent the supplicants on a mission:
assassinate a rival head of state,
surely suicidal proposition.
This Eva West was all that stood between
mad Oz and his insane lust for power.
If she could be removed, then he would win
control over her territory vast;
and if Dorothy and friends should chance to fail,
imprisoned for life they would surely be,
possibly executed for treason:
and either way, no longer his concern.

To much surprise, the friends against all odds
defeated Eva West with sneak attack:
crept past the flying monkeys who stood guard,
surprised her where she stood in her own house.
They trussed her up and tossed her in a pond
where beneath the surface struggling she sank
and in the muddy water drowned, alone.

So Dorothy, now a double murderer,
went back in triumph to see Mayor Oz;
and he, alarmed that now he'd be required
all his empty promises to fulfill
blustered and thundered and excuses made
until finally little Toto's barking
revealed the man behind the curtain green,
exposed the "wizard" as a charlatan.
Desperate now to get rid of these five foes,
Oz made some shit up: with gaslighting said,
"That which you seek, you have had all along!"
then climbed into an air balloon and fled.

Sad Dorothy now stranded for evermore,
believed she would never again see home.
But evil Glenda, on her way back South,
stopped by in Em'rald City for the night.
Rememb'ring magic slippers Dorothy had
obtained from dead Eastwitch, Glenda felt greed.
Desiring magic slippers for herself,
to Dorothy Glenda gave, with grudging guile,
words of advice that could have saved so much
if only she had told her at the start:
"There's no need to appeal to the throne:
just click your heels and say, 'No place like home!'"

Then Dorothy was transported out of Oz.
Glenda imprisoned her friends, just because.

Now you have heard the story, this one's true:
so much depends upon your point of view!

Johnny Appleseed

A story I would like to tell today
about a man who once did something great.
No, he was not involved in politics;
some say he was just a bum in the sticks.
Important he became for planting trees:
the legendary Johnny Appleseed.

This Johnny Appleseed he wandered far,
across the land (he did not have a car)
and brought with him the seeds for which he's named,
he planted them in wilderness untamed.
He planted apple trees on hill and vale,
and round the campfire he would tell a tale
about how he had learned to love the trees
in this his home, the great land of the free.
(Just what his tale was, I now wish I knew;
if I made one up, it would not be true.)

They told me about Appleseed in school;
recall I little, for I am a fool:
so in the interest of this tall tale
I researched him on Internet's fire sale!

John Chapman was his name when he was born,
he was well-loved for kindness and for more.
He wore a cooking-pot upon his head,
he gratefully accepted floor for bed
when he would tell his stories quite all right
and stay in strangers' houses for the night
as used to be the custom in those days
before people were so fearful always.

He was a man of deep godly beliefs,
and as he wandered, to the folks he'd preach
about behavior that becomes a man
and the best ways of caring for the land.

Horse-loads of seeds he planted, yes, it's true:
so many seeds they filled up two canoes!
From cider-pressers he collected seeds,
and in this way, he got them all for free.

Some say Johnny Appleseed liked to drink
hard apple cider, and this made him think,
"Apple trees should be spread across the land
  so cider hard will always be at hand!"
Some say that's not perfect altruism,
but I think it's nearly communism,
and for that there's still much credit due him.
For once the trees were planted, fruit would grow
for any passer-by to eat, you know:
and giving food to strangers who pass by
the model is of generosity.

It seems likely from how he is described,
he was disturbèd in his frame of mind;
and yet he was so gentle, truly kind,
that friendly faces he could always find.

So from Johnny let us example take
of how a better world we all might make:
with kindness to each other we may please,
and show love to the Earth by planting trees!

Paul Bunyan

There was a man named Bunyan, first name Paul,
he's the subject of many stories tall.
He's reputed a logger to have been,
the biggest clear-cut man you ever seen.
He was so fast and strong at cutting trees
that only stumps remained above his knees.

Babe the Big Blue Ox pulled Paul's heavy loads
such a strong beast, he straightened out the roads!
Between his horns fit forty axe handles;
his giant ox balls caused many scandals!

As a giant in stature reputed
the story has not been refuted
     how Paul, dragging his axe,
          carved Grand Canyon – his tracks!
But don't ask why the river's polluted...

Need a forest leveled? Paul Bunyan can!
With every tree stump beveled? He's your man!
But need the land replanted? Oh, um, wait...
Reforesting is where he's not so great!
Paul Bunyan is no conservationist;
he's just another individualist.

It's true that being huge is really cool;
that's why Paul Bunyan is mentioned in school:
but even if half the stories were true
he's still not a good example for you.

John Henry

John Henry was a great man
who said, "I'll do what I can!"

He tried to out-work a machine,
but a man's not driven by coal or steam.

Now John Henry is dead
and we use machines instead.

Moby Dick

Call me Ishmael! All hands are against me
just like the Biblical figure of old.
I was a sailor on a whaling ship,
the *Pequod* named. We sailed the Seven Seas
in cruel pursuit of innocent quarry,
majestic whales we slaughtered for blubber,
for spermacetti oil and ambergris,
and in this way we hoped fortune to earn.

My best friend on this journey was Queequeg,
a harpooner, a Black man, a Pagan –
I used to mock him, in a joking way,
and accuse him of cannibalism:
for, let's face it, I was a bit racist;
but Queequeg was the kindest mariner
it ever was my privilege to ship with.

Our captain was a madman named Ahab
who rarely from his quarters had emerged,
instead allowing his First Mate Starbuck
to supervise daily operations
and task the crew with orders on our way.
This Captain Ahab an obsession had
which he could not release, it gripped him so:
to him, it meant far more than life itself;
his life's purpose was set upon revenge!

The object of his hatred passionate
was a white whale, who men called Moby Dick:
a most formidable adversary
who had the Captain's former life destroyed.
He'd lost a limb: the whale bit off his leg!
It was an injury that would not heal;
his wounded mind, worse than physical pain.

Thus after our labors had filled the hold
and back again to port we should have turned,
instead, based on a sighting, the madman
sent us to stormy seas far from our homes
the whale to chase, to chase that fucking whale;
to chase the whale, to chase white Moby Dick!
And we, obeying orders and commands
did validate his moods, enable him,
his madness to pursue to the world's end
where found we at the last great Moby Dick!
Mad Ahab then tried to harpoon the whale,
but Moby Dick, albino whale so vast,
the *Pequod* to a thousand pieces smashed:
staved in our wooden ship, and down it sank –
while Ahab by the harpoon rope was lashed
t' th' body of his hated enemy,
united with his obsession in death –
the death to which he had led all his crew,
the death which claimed them all, except for me,
who rescued was, and carried to safety
by coffin empty, a symbol of death:
tho built by Queequeg, it kept me alive.

Alice in Wonderland

'Twas on a sunny day just like today,
the air was hot and still in summertime.
Down by the river on the grass they sat:
bored Alice and her book-reading sister.
With neither hobby nor a book to read,
Alice grew sleepy, and began to doze
when suddenly she was surprised to see
a rabbit white, that ran across the mead
only to pause and cry that he was late.
The time he checked upon a pocket-watch
which he withdrew from his patterned waistcoat.

"Why is a rabbit wearing a waistcoat?"
asked Alice to herself. "It's much too hot
  for clothing, worn over warm rabbit fur!
  This makes no sense at all. I must learn more!"

Then like Ahab, pursuing the white whale,
Alice followed the rabbit down its hole;
by curiousity driven to chase,
rather than vengeance and obsessive hate:
but just as reckless in its consequence.
Surprising as it is that Alice fit
her body through a hole that rabbits made,
'twas more surprising still when down she fell

and plummeted deep into the Earth's bowels.
But falling strangely seemed to take much time
and though deep underground she still could see
the walls of this deep pit, with cupboards lined
and wainscoting and flowered wallpaper
like a bizarre Victorian kitchen.

At last she landed, luckily unhurt,
just barely in time the rabbit to see
as through a small door in the wall he slipped
but closed and locked it behind him. Oh, no!
Alone poor Alice found herself, alone
in a strange fancy hall deep underground
with doors, past which a garden grand she glimpsed
when through the keyhole she managed to look;
but alas, the doors were locked, every one,
and quite too small to pass through, anyhow.
Alice despaired, but then a table saw,
upon which had been placed a fancy key,
and beside it a vial of some liqueur
hung with a tag. Its letters read, "Drink Me."

Now, children, if you're ever in a place
that's far from home and filled with people strange,
it's best to ask just what is in the glass
before you go 'round drinking down some stuff.
But Alice was trusting, and feeling strange
already, and so she just drank it down.
Then as she stood, the walls began to shift
and table next her like a mushroom grew,
its table top the cap above her head,
shooting into the sky like a tall tree;
and then she realized it was she who'd shrunk,
smaller and ev'ry moment smaller grew
until she found herself quite small at last
and trotted happily to the small door,
ready to go through it to the green park

which, through its keyhole, she had seen a glimpse –
when with a gasp she realized that the key
was still sitting upon the table top!
She was now small enough to pass the door,
but far too small to reach up for the key!
She tried to climb the table leg. Alas!
She could not get a grip, and slid back down.

She sat down in despair upon the floor
when unexpectedly she found at hand
a plate of cookies with another tag
quite like the first, but this one "Eat Me" read.
Alice, guessing that they would make her large,
ate some to help her grow back up
so she'd be tall enough to fetch the key.
But these cookies were strong: she went way up
ever so high, up high above the ground.
Although the key now she could reach, alas,
she was too large to pick the damn thing up!
Now quite upset was she, and gave great sobs;
the tears rolled down her cheeks, they splooshed and splashed
upon the ground, and soon a puddle formed,
when Alice saw the beaker of liquid
and managed to a small sip from it drink.

Quickly she shrank, until she was so small
that she upon a lake of tears did float,
her own tears that she'd cried when she was large –
a strangely metaphorical swimming!
The lake of tears became a river, flowed
under a door and out into the land
beyond the strange large hall at the bottom
of the strangest rabbit hole in the world.
Adventures had she many on that day,
and stories heard she from strange characters
after they from the flood of tears had climbed.
They danced and raced and terrible jokes told.

"Why, you should take a porpoise with you, then:
because you never should go anywhere
without a porpoise!" some mad jokester punned.

Wand'ring away from this party at last,
she met a lizard person with a house
who called her "Mary Jane," and so she ate
another of the cookies, and grew large
enough to quarrel with a nesting bird.
Then once again she drank the tincture down,
and down she shrank, deep into her own self,
so small, the blades of grass towered o'er her head.
She wandered through the fields, just insect-sized.

Then she upon a caterpillar came,
the strangest caterpillar ever seen.
It sat upon the cap of a mushroom;
so languidly it lounged, it was placid
as it took great pulls from a long-stemmed hookah,
blew out the smoke, then took another pull,
blew out more smoke, then took another pull.

"Who are you?" the caterpillar asked her
as it gazed down from its mushroom cap seat
with bleary red bloodshot eyes and blank face.

"I'm Alice," she tried to explain, "at least,
I think I am; but I'm no longer sure
if I'm still the same person who I was
when I woke up this morning. Much has changed."

The caterpillar stared at her blankly.
"Who are you?" it asked again, quizzically.

Unsure was Alice if it had forgot
that she'd already introduced herself
or if there were some deeper answer sought;

so she recited children's poetry,
snatches of rhyme with meaning quite obscure
and made a silly fool out of herself
trying to placate the caterpillar
who all the while smoked and smoked, smoked and smoked
on its hookah pipe, and blew out great clouds
with a strange sweet smell and an acrid bite.
The hookah smoke began to fill the glen,
and Alice shook her head, she felt it buzz
as from the second-hand smoke she got high.

"Eat more mushrooms," said the caterpillar.

"I beg your pardon?" in bewilderment
Alice queried the queer caterpillar.

"Mushrooms are the answer," it repeated
as about its head wreaths of hookah smoke billowed
and almost seemed to form the shapes of shrooms.

"Unlikely," Alice said dubiously.

"Of course," the caterpillar calmly quipped.
"They make you short, they make you tall, and more,
  they spin you 'round and 'round until you're lost –
  and when you really don't know where you are,
  that's where, at last, you will find your true self."

And with that, the caterpillar transformed:
burst into being as a butterfly,
its brilliant wings of bright blue unfurled,
and off it wheeled, so high into the sky.

So Alice on the shroom began to gnaw,
on one side first, and on the other next,
until at last she felt just about right
and set forth to explore and find her way

to the garden, or home, she cared not which.
Instead, she found herself at a party.

Some weirdos were seated at a long bench.
One madman wore a top hat far too large;
another guest was mad as a March Hare;
the third, a sleepy Dormouse, fell asleep:
he could not stay awake, he'd had too much
fun that day at the roving Tea Party.

Alice boldly walked up to the table
and joined the Tea Party uninvited.
In response, the Mad Hatter cried, "All right,
 it's time to switch places, everybody!"
So the guests all played some "Musical Chairs."
Alice found herself with a dirty dish,
and began to quarrel with her mad host
regarding manners and propriety
and other sundry niceties, until
the Dormouse launched into a boring tale
so soporific, he put himself to sleep
and everyone lost the thread and chilled out.

After this zany Tea Party, Alice
had a number of adventures, and met
many colorful characters, such as
the Cheshire Cat, maddening, perplexing,
speaking in riddles and nonsense always,
meanwhile pretending to be so helpful,
smiling an aggravating smile so broad
it made her want to punch him in the face,
but that was very difficult because
he smiled so broadly that he disappeared.

At last, at last, at long last, Alice found
her way onto the greenway she had seen
when she peeped through the keyhole in the hall
after she first chased that damn Rabbit White.
The strange gardeners were painting roses,
and the haughty Queen ordered them all killed
(her small docile husband, the King, spared them).

Then Alice did the Queen of Hearts invite
to play a game of croquet, and she tried
her best to play along; but Wonderland
had the strangest sorts of game equipment,
with palace guards standing in for the hoops,
flamingos instead of mallets, poor things,
and hiding hedgehogs in place of the balls:
none of which made any sense; all of which
made croquet rules nearly impossible.
The Queen seemed intent on executing
the competition just to win the game
and every moment screamed, "Off with their heads!"
She canceled more people than Robespierre!

At last, despite all this rank injustice,
the royal court decided to go to court.
The Knave of Hearts was given a show trial
as he stood accused of eating some tarts.
Nobody present seemed to understand
the rules of evidence; or procedures
for deposing witnesses as they gave
testimony; or cross-examining.
The jury members could not figure out
what trial evidence was unimportant,
or what was going on in the first place.
Bill the Lizard Person stood on his head;
Alice remarked he was just as useful
with his ass-end up as the other way.

This farcical trial had gone on some time
when the shrooms Alice had eaten kicked in.
She began to feel too large for the room,
so much larger than anyone else there,
hugely disproportionate she had grown
and all of the silly authorities
shouting 'bout petty trivialities
became so irrelevant, she just laughed.
Alice laughed at them, laughed in their faces,
laughed at the useless King, the haughty Queen,
and at the ridiculous White Rabbit.
She cried out, "Why, this is only a game!"
which for some reason upset them greatly,
and they all flew at her, flew in her face,
which is when she woke up. They were just leaves
falling on her face. It had been a dream!

All of Wonderland was only a dream,
and Alice found herself still sitting there
beside her sister on the grassy banks
of the lazy river beneath the trees
on that sunny summer day, like today.

Casey Jones

Casey Jones once rescued a little girl
who had stopped on the train tracks, petrified,
too terrified to get out of the way
as the locomotive barreled towards her.
Jones happened to be oiling relief valves
when he saw the child who'd stopped on the tracks.
He shouted to his fellow engineer,
"Throw it into reverse, Bob, quickly now!"
and raced forward along the running board
to the cattle catcher at the train's front.
He clambered out to the tip of the train
as it approached the petrified small child.
Perched, clinging tight to the front of the train,
he leaned forward over the railroad tracks
and stretched forth his arms to pluck the young child
out of harm's way at the final moment,
swinging her onto the train that she feared
a mere fraction of a second before
the story would have ended tragically
had Casey Jones not been so brave that day
and fearlessly risked his own life to save
a complete stranger from Fate's certain death.
But that act of heroism is not
what Casey Jones is best remembered for.

It's for the way he died his name lives on,
the most famous of the steam engineers.
It matters not if he was sleep deprived,
his work was top notch anyway.

(He certainly was not high on cocaine,
 as the Grateful Dead in their version claim;
 they just said that because it rhymes with "train"
 and not because there's truth to that refrain!)

But true it is, 'twas late into the night
as Casey Jones was at the train's controls.
He did not see flag-waving signal man
obscured by fog and night – the train sped on,
the train they called the Cannonball, so fast
did it hurtle along the railway line,
and Casey Jones meant to make up lost time
to compensate for late departure;
for by getting his runs to the station
on time, he would someday advancement earn,
or so he hoped – and so he sped, too fast –
yes, Casey Jones was known to be reckless.

Seventy-five miles per hour 'round the curve
the Cannonball careened, when through the rain
emerged the shape of train cars suddenly:
a freight train, stalled, stuck, and stationary
there on his line, in front of his own train;
and the passing track had been occupied
by double-header freight train 83
and infamous freight train 72.
His path they blocked. He knew what he must do.

Though he instructed his colleague to jump,
he did not even think to run away,
but pulled with all his might on the air brakes,
and threw the engine's throttle in reverse
so braking pow'r from the engine he'd gain.
Wheels locked, the train skidded along wet tracks,
Casey wrestled with the controls and tugged
with all his might upon the brake lever
even as he saw the stalled cars approach.

Casey's steam engine plowed through four freight cars,
but ultimately he was successful
in slowing the train. There was but one death.
All the passengers aboard that train lived.
The only person who died on that night
was the bravest of railway engineers:
Casey Jones, who saved a train full of folks
at the cost of his own life. What a guy.

Sherlock Holmes

"I observe from the scratches on your shoes,"
said Sherlock Holmes with great pomposity,
"your lefthanded servant girl is lazy,
 and you walked through the mud three weeks ago."

"My dear Holmes," said Dr. Watson surprised,
"you're wrong in every important respect.
 I walk through the mud almost every day
 but never with knife remove it from shoes,
 and nobody has a servant girl, man,
 do I look like a wealthy aristocrat?"

The Headless Horseman of Sleepy Hollow

Sleepy Hollow was a country village
up in the hills some two miles from Greensburgh,
a market port locals call "Tarry Town."
No market nor port had Sleepy Hollow,
just languid summer days, long winter eves,
and superstitious folks to gossip prone.
They gossiped 'bout the widow and the priest,
they gossiped 'bout the drunkard and his wife.
They gossiped 'bout the lanky schoolmaster,
beaky stork-limbed fellow, Ichabod Crane,
an educated man from out of town
who was given to beating his students
with a birch-rod cane to impose order.
And they gossiped 'bout a certain soldier,
a German mercenary in the War,
that valiant struggle for Independence
the States had won just thirty years before.
This German mercenary, so they said,
had, in a battle, lost his very head
when Yankee rebels with a cannonball
had smacked it from his shoulders as he rode
his horse into the fray for old King George
(or, more properly, for George's money).
Thus suddenly deprived of his head,
the horseman's corpse was buried; but though dead,
his ghost often arose from the graveyard,
and through the night rode, seeking near and far
for that precious head, which he had misplaced
(it splattered like a melon, left no trace).

At least, that was the story townfolks told;
and one must never question the gossips,
lest the gossips should turn their tongues to you!
But in the sunny daytime no one thought
about the headless Hessian or his ghost.
Their talk turned instead to one another
and in their boredom, aroused suspicions,
invented narratives, and stoked hatred:
the favored pastimes of the small-minded.

These gossips, lazy idlers that they were,
remarked upon the fact that Ichabod
(who had made himself a reputation
 for behaving quite diff'rently where he lodged
 and at the social ladies' tea parties,
 showing far more kindness than at his school)
had taken it into his simple head
to court a young woman well-known in town:
one Katrina Van Tassel, a local lass
in both her features and her fortunes fair.
To the Van Tassel farm the schoolmaster
himself betaken had, many an eve,
the young lady's company to enjoy –
and the well-furnished dinner table, too.
But quite a catch was she, and had many
admirers all competing for her hand,
including burly Abraham, "Brom Bones,"
a bully, backed by buddies and fists both,
who got away with anything at all,
because the locals said, "He's on our side!"
When this Brom Bones noticed that Ichabod
had gained lovely Katrina's favor fair,
his jealousy and ego were inflamed
and haply would have brawled, given the chance.
Avoiding altercation, Ichabod
instead became the target of campaigns
of pranks, harassment, and nasty rumors.

One night, Katrina's father held a ball,
a local shindig, jamboree and dance
to celebrate the Harvest and the Fall,
and all of Sleepy Hollow would go thence.
Well, Ichabod put on his only suit
and to the party rode a borrowed horse,
looking quite ridiculous, had he known.
Upon arriving, hungry Ichabod
his plate piled high with fruit pies and roast beef,
then filled his gullet up with fine strong beer
and soon with flushèd cheeks felt in good cheer.
He asked lovely Katrina then to dance,
and, with her, floaty-flopped over the floor.
After the song's end, Ichabod retired
to take a breather with some older men
in a warm corner, reciting legends
and telling tall tales of local flavor.
Inevitably the dismal tale was told
(among many others of ghosts and ghouls)
of how the Headless Horseman rode the roads
seeking always replacement for his head.

Now late at night, the people all went home,
but Ichabod, for love the last to leave,
appeared crestfallen as he left the house –
Katrina's favor having wandered off,
to him denied the evening's parting kiss.
Rejected Ichabod mounted his horse
and through the dark trees t'wards his lodging rode.

All full of terrors was the damp dark night
through lonely woods beneath a starless sky,
the clopping of his horse's hooves absorbed
by moss and piles of dead decaying leaves.
Now nervous, Ichabod began to hum,
his jagged nerves to soothe with a soft tune,

as he rode past landmarks of ill repute
of which tales had been told at evening's end.
He kicked his horse as they approached a bridge,
hoping to cross and be swiftly away.
Instead, the beast ran him into a fence
and from thence plunged into a bramble patch.
Now Ichabod was truly filled with fear,
for there was danger that his horse might bolt
and throw him into thicket, over ledge,
or in the swampy brook, where he might drown.
Trying to impose his will on the horse,
the schoolmaster glanced back up to the road
and to his horror saw a figure there,
fearsome and huge, yet only partly seen.

"And who are you?" asked Ichabod in tones
that would have made a mouse chuckle to hear,
poor Ichabod so squeaked in fearful fright.

The figure as for answer made it none,
but stood forth upon the lonely dark road
into a patch of soft moonlight to show
himself a giant on horseback, with no head!
Now Ichabod at once recalled the tale
of Horseman Headless riding through the night.
When he regained the road, our hero rode
as fast as his surly old mount would run,
but his pursuer chased him down the lane.
His horse was spooked, and it the wrong way ran
away from town, deeper into the woods,
and always close behind them rode the steed
of the ghostly headless mercenary.

He rode so hard the saddle quite fell off;
perhaps he had not cinched it tight enough
for such exertion as this midnight ride.
At last he crossed a bridge at the far side

of marshy lowlands just before the church.
Turning, expected he Horseman to see
dissolve into thin air, flashing in flames.
Instead, the Horseman in his hand upheld
his head, somehow retrieved that night from Hell,
and hurled it at the hapless Ichabod!
It struck him in the side of his soft skull
and from his horse he tumbled to the ground.

Poor Ichabod was never seen again.
Though some would claim he'd simply slunk away
after his dual humiliation night,
the knowing housewives all were quite agreed
that Ichabod had been taken away
by spirits of the dead, risen from Hell –
smashed pumpkin, all that in his place remained!
Brom Bones, who soon Katrina marrièd,
was seen to laugh aloud at this strange tale,
but ne'er the narrative contradicted:
for everyone knows, never contradict
the narrative favored by the gossips
lest you become their next target yourself!

Cinderella

The tale of Cinderella
    is not the version we all know.
The story we all remember
    is from a Disney show!

Try it tonight, read Brothers Grimm,
    you'll think, "This is some other
story of Cinderella, surely:
    for *where* is the fairy godmother?"

Yes, I checked in my translation
    and was surprised to see it's true.
The original words have just some birds;
    and no glass slipper – just a shoe!

Above all, quite astounded was I
    when I from that old book did learn
the fable had no magic carriage bright
    that to a pumpkin would return!

For growing up, the carriage pumpkin
    its stem a-sprouting those green vines
was a common family metaphor
    for the importance of deadlines.

But in the early version
    written down by Brothers Grimm
the real evil is Cinderella's father –
    I don't think much of him.

For on the wicked stepmother
      and on her daughters two
is heaped disdain and rage aflame;
      but what did the father do?

He married the bitch, and brought her home,
      and saw his own daughter abused.
His new wife took the child's clothes and bed away;
      and this behavior, he excused!

There is no doubt the father knew.
      It's clear he was aware;
for when the Prince came to fit the shoe,
      the *father* said no one else was there!

Yes, Cinderella's father was
      so morally decayed,
her very existence he denied,
      and his daughter he betrayed.

Yet in the story's moral end,
      the retribution, karma, fate,
only the step-sisters suffer
      for their deeds, now that it was too late!

The father and the step-mother
      were never called to account
for their role in this terrible story
      because "justice" is fiction, in any amount!

A Christmas Carol

Is the tale of Ebeneezer Scrooge
        intended to inspire?
Is there truly anyone for whom
        avarice is their sole desire?

The few for whom the tale is meant
are quite unlikely to repent
if all their whole lives they have spent
greedily piling cent on cent.

In greedy Ebeneezer Scrooge
        are we meant to see ourselves?
Do you toss out mailed solicitations
        while you have food upon your shelves?

Do you feel as though you've given
        everything you can
while everyone in the whole wide world
        comes up with outstretched hand?

Perhaps your massive debt burden
        is squelching your cash flow?
Remember: of other people's lives
        there's much that we don't know.

It always is so easy
        for us haughty to tell
some other person far away
        that they're going to Hell.

We must fight the temptation
        to judgment to give in
and inspire through our example
        rather than accusing of sin.

As inspirational stories go
        I think it rather strange
we rely on inciting guilt
        when we want others to change.

In Ebeneezer let us see
        a hopeful tale of life transformed
rather than allow ourselves to dwell
        upon dismissive scorn.

In truth, when you guilt-trip most folks
        they tend to double down.
No, guilt in fact is a real sad act
        if you want someone to come around.

Although I love the story more
        than this poem might indicate,
if *you* write the next "Christmas Carol,"
        be positive, and celebrate!

The Fruit Seller's Tale

A tale is told on dark evenings
    about a man with a fruit stall
who performed an experiment
    on his customers, one and all.

He took two identical bunches of grapes
    and sold them side by side.
He put different labels upon each bin –
    but both of those labels lied!

For one of those bins was labeled "Us"
    and "Them" the other label read;
and the bin labeled "Us," it sold out fast,
    while the other was left for dead.

The name it mattered not at all,
    for the grapes were just the same:
some were juicy, and some were flawed;
    yet people chose based on the name.

So the Keeper tried again, as a trial now and then,
    with the *same fruit* labeled "Good" or "Bad" –
and everyone complained about the "Bad"
    but they said "Good" was the best they'd had!

Yet another effect the shopkeeper noticed
    as he tried this again, over time:
because no one ever bought the grapes labeled "Bad,"
    those ones rotted on the vine.

Yes, the label predicted the outcome,
    for it told the people what to do.
Because they believed what the label said,
    eventually they made the name come true!

Rip van Winkle

*This poem is dedicated to Bo Mandoe / "Ned Rage Garden"
who suggested the idea of a Rip van Winkle retelling.*

That day, when Rip van Winkle took a walk
into the nearby forest to hunt deer,
he had no premonition of the change
that soon he would find wrought upon his life.

A simple man with simple joys and tastes,
van Winkle hailed from Pennsylvania old.
When he was a young man, he'd fought the French
and allied Native forces in the war
that lasted seven years, and changed the course
of histōry, as wars so often do.
He'd learned to shoot a musket, and to drink
as soldiers learn to drink, around the fire
in camp between engagements and patrols.
Now sev'ral years had passed, and he was just
another vet'ran with PTSD
undiagnosed, from all that he had seen.
So to escape his thoughts he wandered out
into the forest on that fateful day
in search of venison to make some stew,
in search of quiet for his jangled nerves,
away from noisy children and shrill wife:
into the woods, where he could be alone.

But as he searched in vain for a great buck
that he could carry home in victory,
van Winkle heard a thund'ring from the rill
and curious he grew. So down he went,
descending to the far side of the ridge
into a glen which he'd not seen before,
although he'd walked these woods for his whole life.
 "That's strange," said Rip van Winkle to himself,
but then that thunder once again broke through
his thoughts, and he pursued it to its source.

He found a lovely clearing where some men
and women who he'd never met before
were holding a grand picnic-carnival
complete with ample barrels of good beer.
The source, it seemed, o' th' thund'rous sounds he'd heard
was some strange form of bowling on the green.
When heavy ball rolled into target pins,
the clatter did resound throughout the woods
and all the people laughed and clapped their hands
as to each other players talked their smack.
Then someone saw van Winkle where he stood
half-hidden in the trees a-by the mead,
and to him called, "Come, sirrah, join our game!"
As one who dreams, van Winkle wandered forth
and introduced himself to those queer folk.

Their clothes and speech seemed quaint, and quite antique
as though from some far distant time they hailed.
He wondered if perhaps the folk were fae,
or leprechauns, or other mythic sorts;
but tho their dress and speech seemed very queer,
they had not pointy ears, nor other signs
identifying them as fairy-folk.
And yet he thought of no questions to ask
but simply took a cup of ale to hand
and relished, as he drank, its frothy taste.

"This is some mighty good beer," he observed.
"A man could lose himself in such a drink."

His hosts burst forth in cackling and guffaws.
Said one, "You know not how true those words be!"

But Rip van Winkle had no urge to ask
deep questions of his strange but gen'rous hosts.
He drank another mug, and soon lost count
of just how many drinks he had enjoyed.

He joined the bowling game, and soon he found
he had some nat'ral talent. What a joy!
He hardly noticed when the sun went down,
but suddenly there was a merry band
of fiddlers, flutes, and drums playing a jig.
Exuberance had swept him up, and he
was far past care or any rational thought.
He danced with women other than his wife
for the first time since his own wedding dance.
Did it go farther? He was never sure
where dreams began, or what in truth was real.
So strange were his experiences that day
when he those strangers met, deep in the woods.

The morning sun shone bright upon his face,
as in the branches birds sang carefree songs.
Van Winkle found himself beneath a tree,
and epic was his hangover that morn.

"I feel as though I'd slept hundreds of years,"
he groaned, and looked about himself to see
what had become of his companions queer
with whom he'd spent the mem'r'le night just past.
But they were not about; he was alone.
"Oh, what a night that was," van Winkle said,

and with his hands he felt his aching head.
Surprised he was to find his arms entwined
by roots and grass stems and encircling vines.
His clothes were crumbling, overgrown with moss,
and there, beside him, resting on his knee
was his best rifle, which he'd brought along
on his deer hunting trip just yesterday –
but he could only recognize it now
by his initials, carved into the stock,
the wood of which was rotted and sun-bleached.
The barrel, noted he with great dismay,
had rusted where it sat, and quite dissolved
in places: flakes that break crumbling away
now soft as paper: 'twas hardly a gun.

"I'll never shoot a deer with this," he moaned.
"What kind of rain fell down on me this night?"
he wondered with an awestruck look about;
for tho the morn was chilly with light frost,
there was no sign of any recent rain.

Surprised he most of all was when he found
with fingertip's astonished disbelief
a mat of fur descending from his face
that seemed to gather 'bout his lap and knees
and yet was deeply rooted in his skin.
"By God," van Winkle cried out, "it's my beard!"

So Rip van Winkle, frightened and afeared,
determined he would rush back to his home
to see his darling wife and perfect kids:
he felt their absence, strong and visceral.
Forth from that glade he strode, but lost his way
quite quickly: he'd not seen these woods before;
'twas certain he'd remember if he had,
for giant were the trees, and strange the shrubs,
as though he'd stumbled into Fairy Land.

But soon as he broke through a farther hedge,
he found a roadway, broad and black and paved
with some strange black stuff he'd not seen before.
"When did they put a road here, in these hills?"
van Winkle wondered as he scratched his head.
Then guessing at the way back to his town
van Winkle wandered down the winding road.

But after a few stumbling miles he'd gone,
he heard a strange sound, as a roaring wind,
approaching from the rear at a great speed.
He leapt back in alarm, and just in time:
for like a cannonball there hurtled past
a huge contraption, rolling on wide wheels,
a carriage bright and broad, with windows clear,
and, strange to see, no horses anywhere.
This vehicle bizarre screeched to a halt
and out the driver leapt, dressed in strange clothes
that showed no sense of pride nor godly life.
In horror and revulsion, Rip van stared.

"Are you okay?" the strange man said to him.
"Why are you standing in the road?"

"Just trying to walk home," van Winkle said,
and gave out the address of his farm house.

The stranger was a good Samaritan
and offered Rip van Winkle a ride home.
But when they got to that address, 'twas gone!
The house had disappeared, and in its place
a shanty-shack apartment dwelling-house
that stood across the street from a strange store
where speakers frequently announced phone calls
and beeps and tones intruded on the peace.

"This isn't it!" van Winkle said, surprised.

Then out the car the helpful driver hopped,
accosting the first person he could find
t' ask, "Do you know this old man in my car?"

So Rip van Winkle fumbled with the latch
until at length he fell out of the car
when underneath his weight opened the door.
Away he slipped, and wandered down the road
amazed at all he saw, where'er he walked.

In time, he was picked up by the police;
a psychiatric eval underwent.
There seemed to be confusion on the date.
The calendar these people used was wrong –
the day, the month; but most of all, the year!

"Is George not still the King?" van Winkle asked.

"You're kidding, right? Who is the President?"
asked the evaluator, quite confused.

"What is a President?" van Winkle said.

"So, do you have a phone number? Cell phone?"
the gentle psych evaluator asked,
concern apparent in her earnest voice.
A while it had been since she last had seen
a patient quite so lost, sad, and confused.
This strange man did not know the century,
and said he was not from th' United States,
yet claimed he had grown up right here, in town:
a likely story, he so clearly was
delusions suffering, psychotic break.

When Rip van Winkle understood at last
that he had been asleep hundreds of years
and everyone he knew had turned to dust
and all the life he'd lived was now long gone,
he broke down and he wept, cried bitter tears
of pity for himself, and for his wife
who must have thought he'd run away from her.
"Oh, my poor children! What must they have thought!"
he wondered, as he watched the plain white walls.

Thus Rip van Winkle was hardly the first
to lose himself in drink, and lose his wife
and family in consequence also.
A night or two have many lost, at most;
but Rip van Winkle lost hundreds of years.

"So, what's it like?" he asked, when time had passed.
"What do you people do? How do you live?"

To which said candidly the friendly shrink,
"Thru ev'ry day at little screens we look,
and in our pockets carry them with us.
They buzz and noises make to us alert
that we to our screens must attention pay
and never too much time allow to pass
before we pay our screens our heed again."

"Then, are you happy, when you look at screens?"
asked Rip van Winkle, puzzled by this news.

"No, not at all," she laughed. "We are upset!
 The screens are always giving us bad news
 and telling us we're victims with no hope.
 They fill us full of shame and fear and hate
 which we upon each other vomit forth
 with posturing, and accusations grand;
 we call each other names, we scream and shout."

"But if you are unhappy from the screens,"
asked Rip van Winkle, puzzled, "why do you
  persist in walking with them ev'rywhere
  and looking at them, as you're doing now?"

"Oh, whoops, heh heh, I'll put that back away,"
the young psychiatrist laughed guiltily.
"You see, van Winkle," she to him explained,
"we are conditioned to keep checking back.
  We all behave like addicts, craving crack;
  we notice when we go without a fix.
  Besides which, no one really wants to quit,
  'cause all our friends are online ev'ry day
  and that's how we communicate with them.
  If anyone signs out, they cease to be!
  Our relevance in life is based on 'Likes,'
  the comments on our content, and the shares.
  Our work and social lives are through web apps.
  Apps choose who we will date, and what we'll buy;
  and algorithms charged with targeting
  determine what we see, hear, and believe."

"That sounds a nightmare," Rip van Winkle said.

"But what a great world it has built for us!"
the brilliant psych professional enthused.
"If anyone says something that offends,
  ten thousand of us will descend at once
  to cancel them: and thus we all defend
  the purity of thought throughout the land.
  Praise freedom!" she said brightly. "We're so free!"

"It sounds like you are pris'ners of the mind,
  as I've been made a pris'ner of your time,"
said Rip van Winkle, who's thereafter doomed
his days to live out in a padded room.

The Bremen Town Musicians

"My load's too heavy, and my days too long,"
complained the donkey. "What is it all for?
  I'd rather spend my time just singing songs!
  I think I shall not do this any more."
With that, he kicked, and broke the stable door.

"There's opportunity in Bremen Town,"
the donkey told himself, as 'way he fled,
"for anyone to turn their life around!
  I want to sing the songs that fill my head.
  My fortune I shall seek in town instead!"

Next morning, as that road he walked along
through thickest bank of chilly morning fog
and to himself he sang a braying song,
the donkey came across a lonely dog
a-curled up near the road, beneath a log.

"I ran away from home," the dog explained,
"because my master beat me day and night.
  I loved the fam'ly, but I was in pain.
  No longer was there any hope in sight
    that someday they would treat me as is right."

"Well, you should join me then," the donkey said,
"for just like you, I've left my home behind
  to seek new life in Bremen Town instead.
  I'm hopeful that my fortune I shall find
    and thus relieve the sadness of my mind."

So dog and donkey set forth on their way
and cheerily they spoke of this and that
until they came upon another stray:
a golden-eyed calico kitty cat
who licked her paws, and nibbled on a rat.

"Well, hello, gentlemen, where goest thou?"
the kitty asked, and blinked her golden eyes.
The dog said, "Bremen Town!" The cat said, "Meow!
  Perhaps to wander with you would be nice."
They asked no story, so she told no lies.

Thus donkey chose to run away from home
and met a dog and cat along the way.
They asked, "What shall we do, as on we roam?"
He said, "I have a talent: I can bray!
  So let us make a band, and we shall play."

"That's great!" exclaimed the dog. "I'll bark in time,
  and if you need a low note, I can growl!"
Said cat, "I'll fill your songs with words that rhyme,
  and fill the chorus with my sultry yowl
  while for a better life we're on the prowl."

Together wandered they down dusty roads
t'wards Bremen Town, to find their fortune there,
until they heard a shocking rooster crow
that echoed through the early morning air
and gave the sleeping birds all quite a scare.

"What brings you to this lonely road, my friend?"
they asked when they had come upon the cock
who'd crowed. They found him just around the bend:
bedraggled feathers stood upon a rock;
he peered about, and of his world took stock.

"Alas, I had to run away from home,"
the rooster said, and heaved a rooster sigh.
"Now through this heartless world alone I roam,
  for to the farm I had to say good-bye:
  they planned to eat me! Though I know not why."

The cat then licked her lips, but she demurred
from saying what was really on her mind.
"Why, you should come with us!" the kitty purred,
"for we are on the path to new life find
  and leave all of our former lives behind."

"Can you make music?" asked the donkey bard,
intent upon the goal they would reach hence –
without a skillset, life would be quite hard!
"I many mornings sat upon the fence,"
the rooster said, "and crowed my cry intense."

"That's great!" the donkey said. "Let's travel yonder
  and make a living singing our sweet songs."
They pictured all how through the streets they'd wander
accompanied by great admiring throngs;
sweet melodies of love would right all wrongs!

The time drew near to bed down for the night.
Just then, they came upon a country home.
But on reflection, something was not right
about those animals, who all alone
did wander wherever they wished to roam.

"Let us," the donkey said, "sing them a song –
  thus their good graces we shall manifest!
  They'll ask us why we walk this road so long,
  invite us in to be their honored guests."
But when they sang, the people were distressed!

The sound from near the road filled them with dread
as caterwaul and braying filled the air –
they thought it was the newly risen dead,
or else perhaps a vicious rabid bear
a-growling and a-shrieking on, out there.

"Perhaps there's no one home, tho there's a light,"
the donkey said, and walked towards the door.
"Yet we must find a place to spend the night!
　And surely there must be room on their floor
　for simple wandering musicians four."

The people of the house through windows fled
when Bremen Town Musicians came inside.
They thought it was invasion of the dead!
So hurried they away, and sought to hide
out in the barn, or whatever they tried.

"We've got it to ourselves," the dog observed,
after around the house he'd gone and sniffed.
"Tho not too long ago I was unnerved,
　now we are in a house, my spirits lift.
　Our turnaround of fortune was quite swift!"

The house was quite a ways outside of town.
The people had no nearby helpful friends.
After the musicians had bedded down,
the people came, intent on violence
which they believed was in their home's defense!

The animals knew not what was going on
when through the door at night owners came back,
who'd been frightened away by the strange song
but now with bravery tried to attack
rather than find themselves of home in lack.

Alas, the animals had no idea
of what in fact was really happening
or that they had inspired such great fear
when with their voices they had tried to sing –
they truly did not know 'bout anything!

They of a sudden found themselves beset
while they were sleeping in the house that night.
But animals are fierce – do not forget!
And they believed that they were in the right;
and so of course they put up a fierce fight.

The donkey kicked one person in the chest,
another by the dog in leg was bit.
Always grumpy when wakened from her rest,
the cat with claws into a third man lit,
who, terrified, screamed out the words, "Oh shit!"

'Twas but one thing the brave rooster could do
(he'd been up in the rafters of the shack) –
into the last woman's scared face he flew:
with beak, feathers, and talons he attacked,
and thus the people were all driven back!

And after this, the owners ne'er came back,
and went they on instead to Bremen Town
where lived they on the streets in state of lack
complaining of their loss and feeling down
as with some hard liquor their sorrows drowned.

And thus the rumor spread – the house was haunted!
So no one ever knocked upon the door.
The Bremen Town Musicians had all they wanted:
so happy, they could ask for nothing more,
enjoying their new house, their songs did soar!

Br'er Rabbit

Well, Brother Fox sure wanted rabbit stew,
but Brother Rabbit still eluded him.

So in frustration, one day Br'er Fox placed
an online order with the ACME Corp.
which promptly brought out for delivery
some chemicals, which Br'er Fox mixed up well.
From the resulting goo he shaped a form
and sat it on a log beside the road,
where he was sure Br'er Rabbit would pass by.
He dressed the thing in clothing; then he hid
just out of sight nearby to watch the scene.
And sure enough, only a few minutes
had passed, when from around the bend downroad
Br'er Rabbit sauntered swagg'ring into view
as though he were in charge of all he saw.
He sang a song aloud of "Dooh Dah" days,
and seemed to have a bluebird for a friend.

But when he came upon the seated form,
the Glue Baby who sat there on the log,
Br'er Rabbit drew himself to his full height
and called a greeting to that figure strange.
"Well, how d' ye do?" Br'er Rabbit tipped his hat.

But that rude Glue Baby said not a word.

Then thinking he deserved some slight response,
Br'er Rabbit said again, "Well, how d' ye do?"

But still the figure seated by the road
said not a word; for it was made of glue.

Then taking some offense, Br'er Rabbit yelled,
"You're being very rude! I greeted you.
 You have ignored my nice polite 'Hello!'
 Now just one final chance I'm giving you
 before to you I teach a lesson grim.
 Now, I said, 'How d' ye do,' man, 'How d' ye do!'"

But still the Glue Baby said not a word.

With that his temper losing, he lashed out!
Br'er Rabbit punched Glue Baby in the face
and instantly became mired in the glue.
He struggled and he punched and kicked and strained,
but ev'rything he did just made it worse.
In time, Br'er Rabbit became stuck so fast
he could not move, could barely even talk.

And seeing this, Br'er Fox 'bout lost control.
"You should have seen your face!" Br'er Fox mocked him,
erupting in loud gales of laughing snorts.
"Now," asked the fox, "what shall I do with you?"

"I do not care," Br'er Rabbit slyly said,
"just please don't throw me in that bramble patch.
 The thorns all look so sharp, they frighten me!"

"Oh, you don't want to be thrown in the thorns,"
Br'er Fox said in a cruèl mocking tone.

"No, anything but that!" Br'er Rabbit cried,
"Oh please, not in the bramble patch, oh please!"

Then where the vines were thickest, and their thorns
as sharp as pointed razors tearing flesh:
Br'er Fox threw Brother Rabbit in that place!

Then gleeful Brother Rabbit cleaned the glue
from off his body with the thorns nearby;
and just before he ran away, he turned.
"Thanks, Brother Fox," he said, "you've saved my life.
 A bramble patch is where I'm most at home!"

In the ancient culture of Western classical antiquity, the story of the Gigantomachy was considered shocking, subversive, even rude. Although the story itself is well-preserved in their artwork, the ancient Greeks considered the subject to be inappropriate for polite conversation. The ancient Romans recognized a similar convention. Thus, when Ovid claims, in the introduction to his book on seduction, that he had been considering writing a Gigantomachy instead, and that he may yet return to the subject at a later time: it is by way of **trolling the reader.** In that passage, Ovid is making an offhand reference to a well-known but offensive and outrageous story, in order to provoke an emotional response from his audience. Ovid never wrote a Gigantomachy; and it seems almost certain that, although he may have briefly toyed with the idea, he never seriously intended to follow through. So it is in honor of Ovid, and in celebration of the kinds of stories that are **so offensive** that people become completely outraged at the very notion that someone might dare to even just so much as mention them: as a rude salute, as a grand but pointless gesture of flipping the bird at society at large, it is my great privilege to present here the broad-strokes outline of this primeval epic tale, in which the giants rise up in rebellion against the gods.

~T.N.

Gigantomachy

"O children," Gaea cried out, "children mine,
    revenge you must take on the gods!
The cruel gods made my darlings prisoners:
    the Titans, chained in Tartarus.
Take vengeance! Punish those who've caused me harm,
    and end the reign of asshole Zeus;
for he doth not deserve to reign o'er Earth
    whose spirit I am. I revolt!"

"O dearest mother," rumbled giant gentle,
    Ephialtes of bright eyesight,
"was it not for rebellion they were cast
    into the pit, and locked away?
Shall we incite rebellion to avenge
    the fate of those who have rebelled?"

"O brother, thy objections must be quelled!"
    Porphyrion rumbled, scowling down.
He was among the strongest of the Giants,
    with Alcyoneus and Typhon.
And tho the Giants were quite leaderless,
    for strength they had utmost respect.
When proud Porphyrion glanced with his grim glare,
    but few would dare stand up to him.
Bright-eyed Ephialtes thus turned away
    and no more he objections voiced.

"Dear Mother," proud Porphyrion turned to her,
    "we all shall join this righteous cause,
and in rebellion 'gainst the tyrant Zeus
    we shall rise up, and throw him down!"

Then all the Giants roared approval loud,
    preparing to march off to war.
Ephialtes closed his bright eyes and shrugged,
    resigned to join his siblings' march.

"We'll kill those asshole gods!" the Giants sang.
    "We shall their thrones seize for ourselves!
We'll kill those asshole gods! We'll throw them down,
    and then the Titans we'll set free!
Our Hundred-Handed brothers, we'll set free!
    One-eyed Cyclopes, we'll set free!
The reign of cruelty will come to an end,
    the prisoners shall be set free!"

When down from high Olympus gazed the gods,
      aghast they were to glimpse the ranks
of Giants on the march! Invaders fierce,
      intent on conquering the throne.

"But we're the good guys!" shrieked the gods aghast,
      "despite the evil we have done!
It's unfair that the Giants should attack,
      no matter who we raped or killed!
For we're the good guys! No one can deny,
      we're rich because we have been *kind*!"
And yet somehow this argument held not
      with those Giants on vengeance bent.

Some say it was the Titans who piled up
      the mountains, to ascend the heights
and on Olympus brazen assault mount
      (just as the Babel builders would);
some credit to the Giants this great feat:
      no barriers could slow them down!
What's certain is the fear that they inspired
      in hearts of gods who'd been thought brave.

When Ares, that most martial god of war,
      espied the Gen'ral at the Giants' fore
he quaked in terror! "We're all doomed!" he shrieked
      and fled the hall in panicked haste -
his lover, Aphrodite, leaving there
      with husband lame and fam'ly mad.

"Perhaps if we are speedy," Hermes said,
      "we can slip past that vanguard fierce,
and with our lives we may escape this day,
      tho we must hide away in shame."

"How dare you," drunken Dionysos derped,
        "suggest that we brave gods should hide?"

Athena shook her head and pointed down
        the mountainside. "Have you yet looked?
'Twould be the course of wisdom to escape,
        so one day we may fight again!
For yonder Typhon wields a strength unknown
        to any hitherto on Earth.
Behold! He comes with eyes of fire bright,
        on legs like tails of serpents stands.
He bellows out a storm cloud in his might,
        and crushes rocks with his bare hands!
Behind him are a thousand Giants strong,
        each one formidable alone:
together, as an army, none could stop
        the onslaught of their weapons fierce."

"I'm sure when mighty Zeus hurls thunderbolts
        he'll send those Giants running back,"
suggested Dionysos. Then he turned,
        and glimpsed almighty Zeus in flight.

"Just save yourselves!" the ruler of the gods
        called back over his shoulders broad.

Thus on that day abandoned they the halls
        which up 'til then had been their home.
They wandered in disguise 'cross lands so far –
        and fled to Egypt to escape!
There, we are told, brave Zeus took on a ram's horns
        and changed his name to Ammon-Ra,
pretentious tho it may have been to claim
        divine affiliation thus!

Of Typhon they were so afeared, they felt
        they all must live under disguise.

And thus Apollo did a thing absurd:
    he wore the feathers of a bird!
Pretended he to be a raven black,
    and people gave him funny looks.

Dionysos swore he'd not be outdone
    and wore the costume of a goat
perhaps in honor of the Satyr-play,
    a satire that mocked tragedy:
because whenever one person is sad,
    another will make fun of them.

Twin sister Artemis, who loved the Moon,
    disguised herself as sleek Bastet.
She wore some clip-on ears and clip-on tail,
    and all the men went mad with lust,
but she ignored them and walked on her way
    pretending that she was a cat.

For Hera, humiliation there was
    when as her rival cow she dressed;
but by the name of Hathor she was known,
    and in time she earned some respect.

But Aphrodite, eyes once filled with love,
    quickly turned into a cold fish
and by the name of Derceto she went,
    wearing a tail like a mermaid.

And Hermes assumed a disguise as well,
    pretending to be ibis-stork.
He changed his name to Thoth, and wisdom taught
    to any who'd listen to him.
Yet few would listen; most just sneered and jeered,
    believing hate was all they'd need.

But living in disguise just could not last,
& nbsp;   and soon enough they were found out.
Then Typhon blew a typhoon in pursuit
    and chased the gods to Sicily.

At last, the gods regrouped and made their stand
    upon the plains still scorched by fire.
There, with a great effort Aetna they raised,
    and then dropped it on Typhon's head –
the fiercest of those Giants they pinned thus,
    and granted new hope to their cause!

"Perhaps," said Ares, "we'll win after all!"
    and crept out from behind his rock.

"We're fighting for our freedom!" chant the Giants.
    "You tyrant gods we shall throw down!"

But Typhon could not lead those troops to war:
    beneath the mountain he was trapped!

"No matter!" cried Porphyrion, "we shall
    the victory achieve at last;
for Typhon was but one of us, and we
    have might aplenty. Raise a cry!"

Then "Hoo-ah!" called the Giants nearest him,
    and clashed their swords upon their shields.

"We're coming for you bastards! Quake in fear!"
    big Alcyoneus did boast.

But without Typhon at the Giants' fore,
      the gods, their courage finding, fought.
The roaring Giants, as they crossed the plain,
      the gods no longer feared so much,
although the Giants flung great boulders high
      and massive oak trees wreathed in flame.

The gods soon found a mortal to stand by,
      defend them in their hour of need.
This feat, not listed 'mong his labors twelve,
      his legend surely did cement:
for Alcyoneus could not be killed
      while he still touched his Mother Earth.
(Anteas was a *doubling* of this tale,
      this story leads me to believe.)
But Hercules did drag the Giant far
      beyond the borders of the land.
Thus Alcyoneus met with defeat,
      which dealt a blow to rebel hopes.

"You'll pay for that outrage!" his brother vowed:
      Porphyrion leapt to attack!
He Hera from her charging courser pulled
      intent on viōlènt vengeance.
But Hercules returned, and shot his bow –
      from Hera then the Giant turned,
and in that moment Zeus fired lightning bolts:
      the fearsome Giant was destroyed!

The greatest Giants now lay in defeat:
      Porphyrion, Alcyoneus;
and monster Typhon, on whom they'd pinned hopes,
      beneath Mount Aetna lay destroyed.
Some Giants now began fearful retreat,
      and this retreat became a rout
as sweeping in, the gods attacked their foes
      and felled them like a forest green!

Then mounting to a horse-drawn chariot
    and taking lightning bolts in hand
great Zeus was joined by Hercules, his son,
    and rode retreating Giants down.
Euboios and Euphorbos fell before,
    trampled to death by horses' hooves.

On foot warlike Athena strode beside
    the coursers four, and smote her foes:
on Enceladus, Sicily she flung;
    Pallas she skinned, hence her title.

But for the gods the victōry was sealed
    when Hercules slew Pankrates.

His *thyrsus* drunken Dionysos flung,
    and with it Eurytos was slain.

Hyperbios and Aganasthes stood
    their ground, but Zeus knocked them to it:
his wrath, unleashed at last, none could withstand;
    they rode the lightning one last time.

To Hera's great wrath Harpolykos fell,
    and never he would rise again.

Poseidon with his trident flung the isle
    Nisyros at Polybotes.

A team of roaring lions, yellow maned,
    drew th' chariòt of Themis just,
as Artemis and Apollo drew bows,
    faced Hyperphas and Alektos.

Hephaestos heated iron to glowing red:
    he Mimas with those missiles killed.

Next magic goddess Hecate stepped forth
    and slew with torches Clytios.

Then Hermes, wearing Hades' magic cap,
    in battle slew Hippolytos;
and Artemis with arrows flying fast
    felled Gration the great. Don't grieve!
The Fates had willed it! They with clubs of bronze
    beat Agrios and Thoön dead.

"O woe," bright-eyed Ephialtes lamented,
    "that we this doom'd quest undertook!"
Apollo's arrow pierced his right eye then,
    and one from Hercules his left.
No longer bright-eyed, Ephialtes fell
    to th' ground, with arrows in his eyes:
Ephialtes, who once had counseled peace
    became a casualty of war.

The Giants had once chased the gods away,
    but all died when the gods returned;
and Gaea, who'd incited rebellion,
    for vengeance thirsting slunk away.

The Trojan War, Part 1

No bards sing deeds of men who stay at home
and clean up cat piss, and cook for the kids;
but those who set forth on adventures grand
are long remembered, their praises extolled:
and such a hero was Ulysses, who
reluctantly set out for distant war
and took a lifetime to return back home.

The light played on the bright green leaves, and cast
soft shadows dancing gaily in the breeze
as overhead the songbirds trilled their tunes,
a commentary on the peaceful life.

When Palamedes called him on the phone,
Ulysses claimed he could not understand.

"Sorry, amigo, you cannot fool me,
  and I know you remember what you said:
  that you would always heed your country's call."

"Of course," Ulysses sighed, "when country calls,
  only a hippie peacenik would decline."

"By Agamemnon summoned you have been,
  the President expects to be obeyed."

"From Agamemnon I will heed the call,
  yet first I'd ask this, before I depart:
  please tell me, what's the cause of all this war,
  and what do we achieve by fighting it?"

"But surely, man, you have heard all the news?"

"Pretend that I have heard no news at all,
  and tell me in your own words why we fight."

"We duty-sworn for Menelaus go:
  an ally's call must rally us to arms,
  else what meaning does an alliance have?
  So it is not our place to question him,
  or ask if Helen should be made to stay
  when it's her right with Paris to depart."

"It's ev'ry person's right to faithless be,
  and ev'ry person's burden to endure
  the consequences of their choices made.
  So why then must ten times ten thousand men
  and women cross the sea to wage a war
  against a country, most of whose people
  had no part in the choice we're mad about?
  What choice had they, in this war that we fight?"

"Why, none at all, and that's the irony!
  Their choices are made for them by the few."

"It's like a story from the tabloid press."

"Perhaps only on one level that's true.
  'Tis whispered that the drama's an excuse:
  that really it's a question of trade routes,
  and who's allowed to levy tax on them;
  plus, there are nat'ral resources at stake.
  The winner of the victory will be

supreme among the nations of the world
for years thereafter, with such benefits
as oft accrue to victors after war.
It is in our strategic interest
to go to war, to slaughter enemies,
and make up any excuses we like.
It is a fine tradition, dating back
before the dawn of modern humankind
and sure to last as long as our species."

Ulysses then shipped off with all his men,
ten ships, well manned, an army on its own:
'twas but a paltry part of that grand fleet.

At first they thought to quickly win the war:
with "Shock and Awe" they would soon overrun
the enemy entrenchments, and they'd teach
those Trojan fools a lesson, yes they would!

Until the war bogged down. Then house by house
Ulysses must pursue his Trojan foes.
The siege and battles lasted full ten years,
and there was bravery done on both sides,
and also traps and treachery and lies:
for in struggles for pow'r, all these are used.
Ulysses, tho good man he strove to be,
felt burdened by some choices that he'd made,
as though he had incurred the wrath of gods.

But Ajax was more often in headlines,
and bold Achilles with his temper fierce;
and Hector, captain of our enemies,
who countered ev'ry move and drove us mad.
For tho the war dragged on, we made no gains,
it was a tit-for-tat game, round and round,
and no side could the victory achieve.

'Til one day on the battlefield, Hector
at last Achilles faced upon the field
of battle, and did fairly him defeat!
It seemed a turning point in that long war.

Then it turned out, to ev'ryone's surprise,
Achilles had not fought at all that day!
He had been sulking AWOL in his bunk
back in the barracks, while his trusted friend
(and rumored lover) Patroclus by name
had in his place been killed. He'd been disguised!
For, as the facts emerged at the inquest,
Achilles had stayed in his bunk to sulk
after a reprimand from Agamemnon;
so Patroclus had led the Myrmidons
(for so named was that company of fame)
in their attack, 'til he came face-to-face
against the mighty Hector, who killed him.
Still as Achilles 'guised, Patroclus fell,
and only later was the truth revealed.

And then Achilles refused to accept
that in this sad event he'd played a role,
because he had refused to leave his bunk
and Patroclus had led his troops instead.
No, all he could think of was Hector's face,
and how he'd squish it, when he took revenge.

Achilles in this manner passed the time,
'til finally he could take it no more
and marched forth into the dangerous zone
between the two encampments, calling out
and naming Hector, saying, "Come out, fight!
  Thou coward who sees fit to slay my friend,
  come see if thou mayst find thy luck to hold,
  or if this is the day when thou shalt die!"

Those heroes twain towards each other fired,
and Hector fell, wounded, in need of aid.

For crimes of looting, torture, kidnapping,
in military prison he was thrown,
Achilles bold, who had sat on his bunk
while life went on outside, to his regret.
Eventually released back to the front,
Achilles died in battle, gruesomely.

The Frame

Dunyazade's Epilogue

Some time had passed, and Dunyazade got bored
of sitting by the bed upon the floor
while she awaited sister's stories more.
She felt it was at last her time to score!
So in the bed she climbed, all unannounced,
and on that murd'rous sheikh at once she pounced!

Sheherazade perhaps was not surprised,
for she had seen the lust in those young eyes.
Together then all three romped through the night,
and all enjoyed those feelings quite all right.

The stories then continued 'til the dawn;
yes, Scheherazade's tales will long live on.

*And they all lived
more or less happily most of the time
ever after, until they died.*

References and Resources

I referenced a number of Wikipedia entries: including articles relating to many holidays; the structure of the modern calendar; the month names of various ancient cultures; Greco-Roman gods and goddesses; historical events; and biographies of historical persons, including Casey Jones and the extended family of Augustus Caesar, among others. I have not cited all of these articles individually, but I thank Wikipedia as an invaluable resource to the layperson who wishes to pursue a variety of interests.

In addition, I gratefully referenced the following resources:

Carroll, Lewis. (1923). *Alice in Wonderland and Through the Looking-Glass.* The John C. Winston Company (The Children's Classics).

Dickens, Charles. (2010 ed.) A Christmas Carol. Audiobook. Duke Classics via Libby.

Doyle, Arthur Conan. (2009 ed.). *The Adventures of Sherlock Holmes.* Narrated by Ralph Cosham. Audiobook. Blackstone Publishing via Libby.

Geras, Adele. (2002). *Troy: A Novel.* Audiobook. Books On Tape via Libby.

Green, Roger Lancelyn. (2006 ed.). *The Tale of Troy.* Audiobook. Blackstone Audio via Libby.

Green, Roger Lancelyn. (2006 ed.) *Tales of the Greek Heroes.* Audiobook. Blackstone Audio via Libby.

Irving, Washington. (ed & intro Austin McC. Fox). (1962 ed). *The Legend of Sleepy Hollow and other selections from Washington Irving: Edited and with an Introduction by Austin McC. Fox.* New York, NY: Washington Square Press (Pocket Books New York, a division of Simon & Schuster, Inc.)

Lucretius. (Ronald Melville, trans.). (2008 ed.). *On the Nature of the Universe: A verse translation by Ronald Melville, with an Introduction and Notes by Don and Peta Fowler.* Oxford, UK: Oxford University Press (Oxford World's Classics).

Melville, Herman. (1976 ed.) *Moby-Dick: or, The Whale. Commentary by Howard Mumford Jones; Text and Notes Prepared by Harrison Hayford and Hershel Parker.* New York, NY: W.W. Norton & Company, Inc.

McCaughrean, Geraldine. (2007). *Odysseus.* Audiobook. Full Cast Audio via Libby.

Osborne, Mary Pope. (2005 ed.) *The One-Eyed Giant and the Land of the Dead.* Audiobook. HarperCollins HarperAudio via Libby.

Ovid. (trans, ed, intro & notes Peter Green). (2005 ed.). *The Poems of Exile: Tristia and the Black Sea Letters, With a New Foreword; Translated with an Introduction, Notes, and Glossary by Peter Green.* Berkeley, CA: University of California Press.

Ovid. (Anne & Peter Wiseman, trans, ed, & notes). (2013 ed.). *Fasti.* Oxford, UK: Oxford University Press (Oxford World's Classics).

Ovid. (trans. A.D. Melville, intro & notes E.J. Kenney; translation of "The Art of Love" by B. P. Moore with revisions by A.D. Melville). (2008 ed.) *The Love Poems*. Oxford, UK: Oxford University Press (Oxford World's Classics). [This rhyming verse translation includes all of Ovid's famous transgressive works of "love" poetry, for which he was later exiled: *Amores, Cosmetics for Ladies, Ars Amatoria,* and *Remedia Amatoria.*]